26x(4)(11) 1/12
31x 11/16 — 8/20

For my good friends John and Helen (and William, Bridget, and Leo)
—M. D.

For Emma, with thanks to Mark McConnell, Lewis Carlei, and Philip, David, and Eileen Pryce
at Cefu Saeson Fawr Farm in Neath
—A. R.

Margaret K. McElderry Books
An imprint of Simon & Schuster Children's Publishing Division
1230 Avenue of the Americas
New York, NY 10020
Copyright © 2002 by Viacom International Inc.
Text copyright © 2002 by Malachy Doyle
Illustrations copyright © 2002 by Angelo Rinaldi
Published simultaneously in Great Britain by Simon & Schuster UK Ltd.
All rights reserved, including the right of reproduction in whole or in part in any form.
Book design by Kristin Smith
The text for this book is set in Minister.
Printed in Hong Kong
2 4 6 8 10 9 7 5 3

Library of Congress Cataloging-in-Publication Data
Doyle, Malachy.
Cow / by Malachy Doyle ; illustrated by Angelo Rinaldi.— 1st ed.
p. cm.
Summary: Illustrations and simple text describe the full day of a dairy cow.
ISBN 0-689-84462-X
1. Dairy cattle—Juvenile fiction. [1. Dairy cattle—Fiction. 2. Cows—Fiction.] I. Rinaldi, Angelo, ill. II. Title.
PZ10.3.D745 Co 2001
[E]—dc21
00-051956

COW

by Malachy Doyle

illustrated by Angelo Rinaldi

Margaret K. McElderry Books

New York London Toronto Sydney Singapore

Cow.

Grazing in the
field on a hot
summer's day.

Early morning.
Dawn is breaking.
The first birds sing,
and the farmer strolls down the lane,

whistling.

Slowly you rise from the sodden grass,
your thick coat wet with morning dew.
Big and heavy,
you amble to the gate,
full udders swinging between your legs.

Past the sheep, resting in their field,
the pigs, dozing in their pens,

the gander, keeping guard,
and the farmhouse, where the children sleep.

Your hooves click on the floor of the yard,
the gate opens, and you enter the stall.

Food drops in front of you,
and you bend to eat.
Gently the farmer cleans your udders
and puts tubes on your teats.
Milk is sucked out—rich, warm,
creamy milk.

Then you wander back to the field.
Past the house, where the children are rising.
Past the coop, where the chickens are laying.

You tear the grass and chew the cud,
rolling your mouth from side to side,
pushing the food with your thick, wet tongue,
over and over
for hours.

The school bus comes for the children,
the tanker arrives for the milk,
and slowly the morning passes.

The day warms up,
and your breath comes hot and heavy
from your broad, wet nose.

You wander down to the river,
and take a long drink of the cool, clear water.

As the midday sun blazes,
you rest in the shade of the oak tree
and close your deep, dark eyes.

Your ears twitch to clear the flies from your face.
You swish them from your back with a long, bushy tail.

The hot afternoon drags on, and the bus returns.
The children come to swing from the tree.
Out over the river,

and *splash!*

into the river.

Later you wait by the gate,
to be first in line,
your milk-full udders aching.

Lowing deeply as the farmer appears.

Pressing forward to the cool parlor at last.

You're back in the field.
The sun has gone.
The flies have flown,
and the long, hot day draws to an end.

You graze,

you chew,

and you rest.

It's hard work
being a cow.